Amazing life cycles
REPTILES
and AMPHIBIANS
by Brian Williams

An Hachette UK Company
www.hachette.co.uk

First published in the USA in 2013 by TickTock, an imprint of Octopus Publishing Group Ltd
Endeavour House, 189 Shaftesbury Avenue, London, WC2H 8JY
www.octopusbooks.co.uk www.octopusbooksusa.com
Copyright © Octopus Publishing Group Ltd 2013
Distributed in the US by Hachette Book Group, USA, 237 Park Avenue, New York, NY 10017, USA
Distributed in Canada by Canadian Manda Group, 165 Dufferin Street, Toronto, Ontario, Canada M6K 3H6

ISBN 978 1 84898 857 6

Printed and bound in China
10 9 8 7 6 5 4 3 2 1

With thanks to Marjorie Frank
Natural history consultant: Dr. Kim Dennis-Bryan F.Z.S
US Editor: Jennifer Dixon   Cover design: Steve West   Production Controller: Alexandra Bell

Picture credits (t=top; b=bottom; c=center; l=left; r=right):
FLPA: 4b, 5t, 6b, 7b, 11b, 17t, 18b, 25t, 25b, 26–27 all. Nature Picture Library: 16b, 19t, 23t, 29t. NHPA: 28–29 main, 31t.
Shutterstock: OFC, 1, 2, 3, 4c, 6t, 8tl, 8b, 9, 10, 12tl, 13c, 13b, 14–15 all, 20 all,22tl, 22–23, 24tl, 24–25b, 30tl, 31b, OBC.
Superstock: 5b, 8c, 11t, 13t, 16tl, 17b,18tl, 19b, 21t, 21b, 30b. TickTock image archive: 4tl, map page 6, 7t.

Every effort has been made to trace copyright holders, and we apologize in advance for any omissions.
We would be pleased to insert the appropriate acknowledgments in any subsequent edition of this publication.

Contents

Words that look
bold like this
are in the glossary.

What is a reptile?

A reptile is an animal with a thick skin covered in **scales**. Reptiles are **ectothermic**. This means that their body **temperature** goes up or down with the temperature of the air or water around them.

This is a crocodile's foot – you can see its scaly skin.

Snakes, lizards, crocodiles, alligators, tortoises, and turtles are all reptiles.

Snakes are reptiles with no legs.

Scales

Every few months, a snake wriggles out of its old skin. A shiny new skin has grown underneath.

Old skin

4

Lizards are reptiles. Most lizards have four legs and a tail.

If a **predator**, such as a bird, grabs a lizard's tail, the tip breaks off. The bird is left with the twitching tail. The lizard runs away and soon grows a new tail!

This agama lizard is growing a new tail – the tip is missing.

Tortoises and turtles are reptiles with shells.

A giant Galapagos tortoise

Reptile life

Adult reptiles usually live on their own. Males and females get together to **mate** and then separate again. After mating, most female reptiles lay eggs, but some reptiles give birth to live babies.

This emerald tree boa gives birth to live babies.

Chameleons are tree lizards that can change their skin color! The female shows the male she is ready to mate by changing color.

AMAZING REPTILE FACT

Most reptile eggs feel rubbery. The shell is softer than a bird's egg, but strong.

A pair of chameleons

Female

Male

Reptiles lay lots of eggs at a time, but not all of them **hatch**. Some eggs fail to develop and some are eaten by other animals.

Female pythons coil their bodies around their eggs to keep them warm.

Most reptile moms leave their eggs to hatch on their own, but some reptiles look after their eggs.

When a baby reptile hatches, it looks like a tiny copy of its parents. The baby is ready to find its own food right away. Baby snakes can hunt as soon as they are born.

Egg

This western pond turtle has just hatched.

What is an amphibian?

An amphibian is an animal that can live in water and on land. Like reptiles, amphibians are ectothermic. Their bodies are the same temperature as the air or water around them. Most amphibians have smooth skin.

This is a toad. It looks like a frog but has drier, bumpier skin.

Frogs, toads, newts, salamanders, and caecilians are all amphibians.

This is a caecilian. It has no legs and looks like a snake.

Newts and salamanders are amphibians with tails.

This is a fire salamander.

Most amphibians like warm, damp places with plenty of plants they can use as hiding places.

AMAZING AMPHIBIAN FACT
The word "amphibian" means "two lives" – one on land and one in water.

Frog and toad tadpoles have tails but lose them when they change into the adult form.

The bright blue color of this poison arrow frog tells predators, "Stay away – I'm poisonous."

Amphibian life

Adult amphibians usually live on their own. Males and females get together to mate. After mating, female amphibians lay eggs. Most amphibians lay their eggs in water. This stops the eggs from drying out.

Amphibian eggs have no shells. A frog's eggs look like jelly.

In the spring, male and female frogs and toads go to ponds to mate. Then the females lay eggs.

AMAZING AMPHIBIAN FACT
The throats of male frogs puff out as they sing a croaky song. This attracts females.

Baby amphibians hatch from eggs. They have large heads and long tails and breathe through **gills**, like fish. Soon they grow legs and begin breathing with lungs. Then they can live on land.

These are the young of a spotted salamander.

Eggs

Most amphibians don't look after their eggs or babies, but there are some amazing amphibian parents.

Some poison arrow frogs lay their eggs in water-filled hollows in trees. If the water dries out, they carry the tadpoles to a new home.

The male midwife toad carries his eggs on his back until they hatch.

Animal habitats

A habitat is the place where a plant or an animal lives. Reptiles and amphibians live in lots of habitats, from warm, wet **rainforests** to dry **grasslands**. Many amphibians live in ponds and rivers in **wetlands**.

The sea is a habitat. Turtles live in the sea.

Reptiles and amphibians live in all habitats except the Arctic and Antarctica.

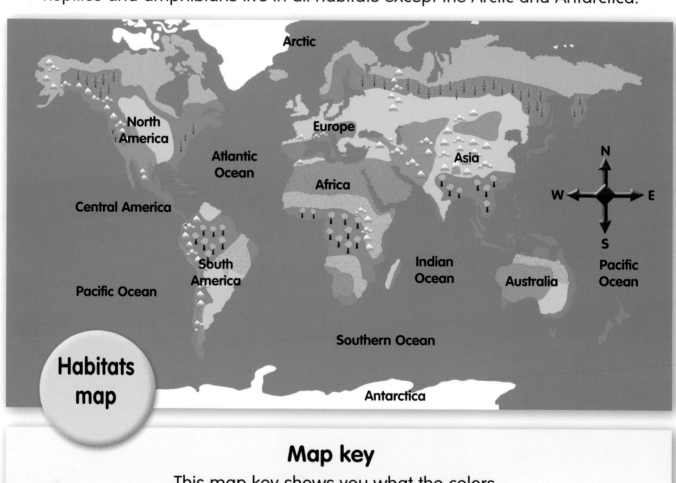

Arctic

North America

Europe

Asia

Atlantic Ocean

Africa

Central America

N

W — E

S

Pacific Ocean

South America

Indian Ocean

Australia

Pacific Ocean

Southern Ocean

Habitats map

Antarctica

Map key
This map key shows you what the colors and pictures on the map mean.

Temperate grasslands – areas that are dry in summer

Tropical grasslands – hot, dry areas with few trees

Arctic/Antarctica – frozen, snowy ground and icy seas

Tundra – cold, windy places

Cool, rainy forests

Cold forests

Warm, wet rainforest

Deserts – dry land with little rain

A marine iguana

Many snakes and lizards live in **deserts**, which can be cold at night. In the morning, they lie in the sun to warm up their bodies.

This thorny devil lizard lives in deserts in Australia.

Marine iguanas live on beaches. Large adult marine iguanas go diving in the ocean to find seaweed to eat.

Tree frogs live in forest habitats. This tree frog's green skin provides good **camouflage** against the leaves. Its color hides it from predators, as well as the insects it hunts.

AMAZING AMPHIBIAN FACT
There may be over 1,000 different kinds of tree frogs.

What is a life cycle?

A life cycle is all the different **stages** and changes that a plant or animal goes through in its life.
The diagrams on these pages show some examples of reptile and amphibian life cycles.

This male Jackson's chameleon uses his horns for display and to fight other males for females.

1 A pair of rattlesnakes

A male and female snake meet and mate.

4 A young emerald tree boa

2 A female corn snake

SNAKE LIFE CYCLE
All reptiles have a life cycle with these stages.

Baby snakes are ready to go off on their own as soon as they hatch or are born.

The female lays eggs. Some snakes give birth to live babies.

3 A baby ball python

Baby snakes hatch from the eggs.

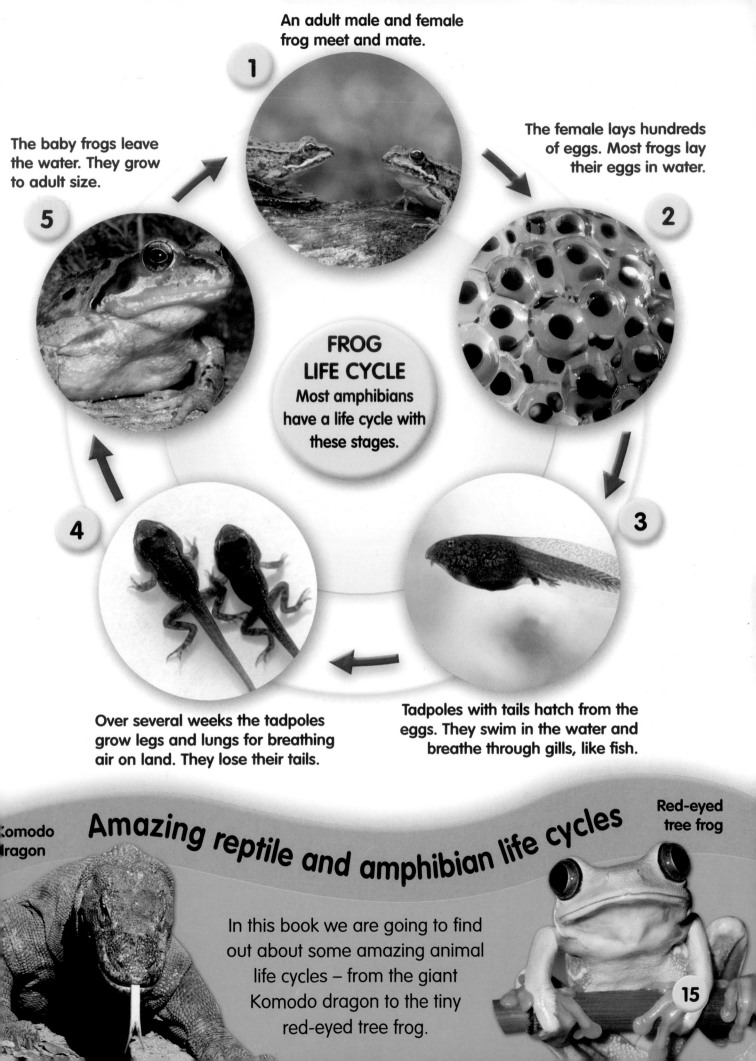

1 An adult male and female frog meet and mate.

The baby frogs leave the water. They grow to adult size.

5

FROG LIFE CYCLE
Most amphibians have a life cycle with these stages.

The female lays hundreds of eggs. Most frogs lay their eggs in water.

2

4

3

Over several weeks the tadpoles grow legs and lungs for breathing air on land. They lose their tails.

Tadpoles with tails hatch from the eggs. They swim in the water and breathe through gills, like fish.

Komodo dragon

Red-eyed tree frog

Amazing reptile and amphibian life cycles

In this book we are going to find out about some amazing animal life cycles – from the giant Komodo dragon to the tiny red-eyed tree frog.

The egg-eating snake
can grow to three feet
(one meter) long.

Egg-eating snake

The egg-eating snake lives on grasslands and in deserts in Africa. The egg-eating snake has no teeth but it can eat a bird's egg, bigger than its head – whole!

The snake's jaws expand...

Egg

...then the snake starts to swallow.

The snake's skin stretches around the egg.

The egg-eating snake has sharp spikes inside its throat, which will crack the shell. Then the snake swallows the yolk and white, and spits out the shell.

A female egg-eating snake lays from 6 to 25 eggs. She lays each egg in a different part of her **territory**. Then she leaves them. The eggs hatch after two to three months.

AMAZING REPTILE FACT
Before eating an egg, the snake touches it with its tongue to make sure it is fresh.

As soon as they hatch, young egg-eaters climb trees to look for eggs.

A crocodile can bite
but it cannot chew.

Nile crocodile

Nile crocodiles live beside lakes and rivers in Africa. They wait for big animals such as antelopes to come for a drink, and then they grab them and eat them! Nile crocodiles also eat monkeys, turtles, birds, and fish.

After about 90 days, the eggs hatch.

After she has mated, the female crocodile makes a nest beside the river. She lays about 60 eggs.

Baby crocodile

AMAZING REPTILE FACT
A male Nile crocodile can grow to 20 feet (6 meters) long.

Crocodiles are fierce, but they are very good moms. They guard their eggs and even help break them open with their mouths so the babies can get out.

The baby crocodiles call to their mom to let her know they are hatching.

The female looks after the babies in the shallow water of the river. After six to eight weeks, the babies go off on their own.

The female gently carries the babies from the nest to the river in her mouth.

An adult green turtle can weigh 660 pounds (300 kilograms).

Green turtle

The green turtle lives in warm oceans. Green turtles eat underwater plants, such as sea grass. Female green turtles go to the waters of the same beach every two to five years to mate and lay eggs.

AMAZING REPTILE FACT

Some females swim about 1,400 miles (2,250 kilometers) to get to their breeding beach. It can take them weeks!

The adult male and female turtles meet and mate in the shallow water.

Turtles swim by paddling with their flippers.

Flipper

The females crawl out of the sea and up onto the beach.

20

The green turtle lays up to 150 eggs on the beach.

The female turtle digs a deep hole in the sand with her flippers. She lays her eggs, covers them with sand, and then crawls back to the sea.

The baby turtles hatch after 45 to 70 days. The babies have to look after themselves. They dig out of the sand and race to the sea.

The tiny turtle hatchlings are in danger of being eaten by predators, such as seabirds.

The dragon's saliva is so full of poisonous germs that just one bite can kill its prey.

Komodo dragon

The Komodo dragon is the world's largest lizard. These giant reptiles live on Komodo Island and two other islands in Southeast Asia. Komodo dragons hunt for almost any kind of animal, including wild pigs, deer, and even buffalo. They also eat animals that are already dead.

Male Komodos fight by standing on their back legs and using their tails for support. The winner mates with the female.

An adult male can be ten feet (three meters) long!

After mating, the female scrapes out a shallow nest in the ground and lays about 25 eggs. The female then leaves the eggs to hatch on their own.

The dragon's eggs hatch after about nine months. The babies climb trees and eat insects and lizards. Trees are safe, because if an adult dragon catches a baby, it will eat it!

This baby dragon is two days old and about 12 inches (30 centimeters) long.

AMAZING REPTILE FACT
A female Komodo dragon in a British zoo laid eggs that hatched into babies even though she had no male around to mate with!

Red-eyed tree frog

The red-eyed tree frog lives in rainforests in Central America. It is a nocturnal frog. This means it rests during the day and is active at night. Red-eyed tree frogs eat insects.

The frog's toes have suction pads that help it stick to leaves as it lays eggs on the underside.

In the breeding season, male red-eyed tree frogs gather together on branches over a pond.

AMAZING AMPHIBIAN FACT

With its eyes closed, the frog blends into its green habitat. If disturbed, it opens its big red eyes – this startles possible predators!

The males call to females with a clicking noise.

This parrot snake is eating a red-eyed tree frog's eggs.

After mating, the female lays up to 50 eggs on a leaf that's hanging over the pond. Laying lots of eggs at a time increases the chances that at least some babies will survive.

After about five days, the eggs hatch, and the tadpoles fall down into the pond below.

Tadpole

When these tadpoles have grown into frogs, they will climb back into the trees.

This frog has an unusual pointy, wobbly section on the end of its nose!

Darwin's frog

The Darwin's frog lives near rivers in damp, shady mountain forests in South America. Darwin's frogs eat insects and small animals, such as worms. The males are very good fathers.

When a female Darwin's frog has laid her eggs, the male guards them. After about two weeks, the babies inside the eggs start to move. Now the male picks up the eggs with his tongue and puts them into his vocal sacs.

The eggs are in here!

The male puts up to 15 eggs into a pouch in his mouth.

The tadpoles hatch inside the male's body. They stay in his body for 50 days, nourished by the attached egg yolk. When they have grown into little froglets, the babies climb out of dad's body!

An adult Darwin's frog is just 1 to 1.25 inches (2.5 to 3 centimeters) long!

Froglet

Axolotl

The axolotl is an amphibian that looks like a baby even when it is an adult. It is a kind of salamander but looks like a giant tadpole. Axolotls live in lakes in Mexico, in Central America, but people also keep them as pets.

If an axolotl loses a leg, it can grow another one.

The axolotl breathes through gills, not lungs, and never comes out of the water.

Gills

The axolotl is 6 to 8 inches (15 to 45 centimeters) long.

Axolotls mate in water. After mating, the female lays up to 1,000 eggs and attaches them to plants and stones.

The eggs hatch in two to three weeks. The babies eat tiny water animals. Their legs start to grow in nine to ten days.

Baby axolotls sometimes eat each other!

Tail

AMAZING AMPHIBIAN FACT
Some people in Mexico like to eat axolotls.

That's amazing!

Are you ready for some more amazing reptile and amphibian facts? Did you know there's a reptile that may breathe only once an hour; a snake that's as long as six men; and a lizard that's a leftover from prehistoric times!

The North American bullfrog lays 25,000 eggs at a time!

These men are carrying an anaconda.

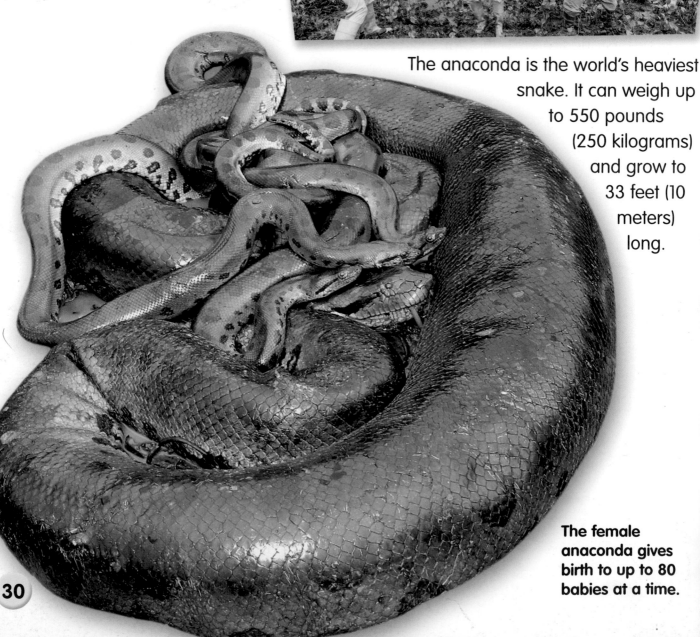

The anaconda is the world's heaviest snake. It can weigh up to 550 pounds (250 kilograms) and grow to 33 feet (10 meters) long.

The female anaconda gives birth to up to 80 babies at a time.

The female Surinam toad lays her eggs and the male puts them onto her back. A protective covering of skin grows over the eggs. When the eggs hatch, the tiny tadpoles remain on the mother's back. After they change into baby toads, they break through the protective covering.

Eggs and baby toads

The tuatara is in a reptile family all of its own. Its closest relatives lived in prehistoric times, among the dinosaurs.

AMAZING REPTILE FACT
When resting, tuataras may take only one breath an hour!

Baby tuataras do not hatch from their eggs for 12 to 15 months – the longest time of any reptile.

Glossary

camouflage – Colors, marks, or a shape that hides an animal from predators and its prey.

deserts – A place where it hardly ever rains. Most deserts are very hot in the day. Some deserts get cold at night.

ectothermic – An ectothermic animal sits in the sun to warm up and looks for shade to cool down.

gills – Breathing organs (parts of the body) in animals that live in water, such as fish and baby amphibians.

grasslands – Wide open grassy spaces with few trees.

hatch – When a baby bird or animal breaks out of its egg.

mate – When a male and female animal meet and have babies.

predator – An animal that hunts and kills other animals for food.

rainforests – Dense forests of tall trees in places with lots of rain.

scales – Hard plates of skin that cover the bodies of reptiles and most fish.

stages – Different times in an animal's life when the animal changes.

temperature – How hot or cold something is.

territory – An area or place that an animal defends and where the animal feeds and breeds.

wetlands – Damp places with wet, boggy ground and lots of ponds, lakes, or rivers.

Index